Emmanuel Cerisier

IN WILLIAM THE CONQUEROR'S FOOTSTEPS

HASTINGS 1066

OREP

EDITIONS

Thanks to Philippe Brochard and Gilles Pivard.

OREP Éditions, Zone tertiaire de Nonant – 14400 BAYEUX
Tel: 02 31 51 81 31 – Fax: 02 31 51 81 32
E-mail: info@orepeditions.com – Website: www.orepeditions.com

Editor: Grégory Pique – Graphic design: Éditions OREP
Layout: Sophie Youf
Editorial coordination: Corine Desprez
English translation: Heather Inglis

French Law n°49-956 dated 16th July 1949 on publications for young readers – April 2016

To Gaspard and Rémi.

In the spring of the year 1066, a
Norman lord named Tancrède de Hautmesnil
left his fief, accompanied by his armed guards, to join the
army led by William, the Duke of Normandy, also known as William
the Bastard. William had decided to raise an army and to conquer
England, because Harold Godwinson had seized the throne that was
rightly William's. Tancrède went to his keep one last time.
According to William's promises, if he should return there one day,
it would be as a rich man covered with glory...

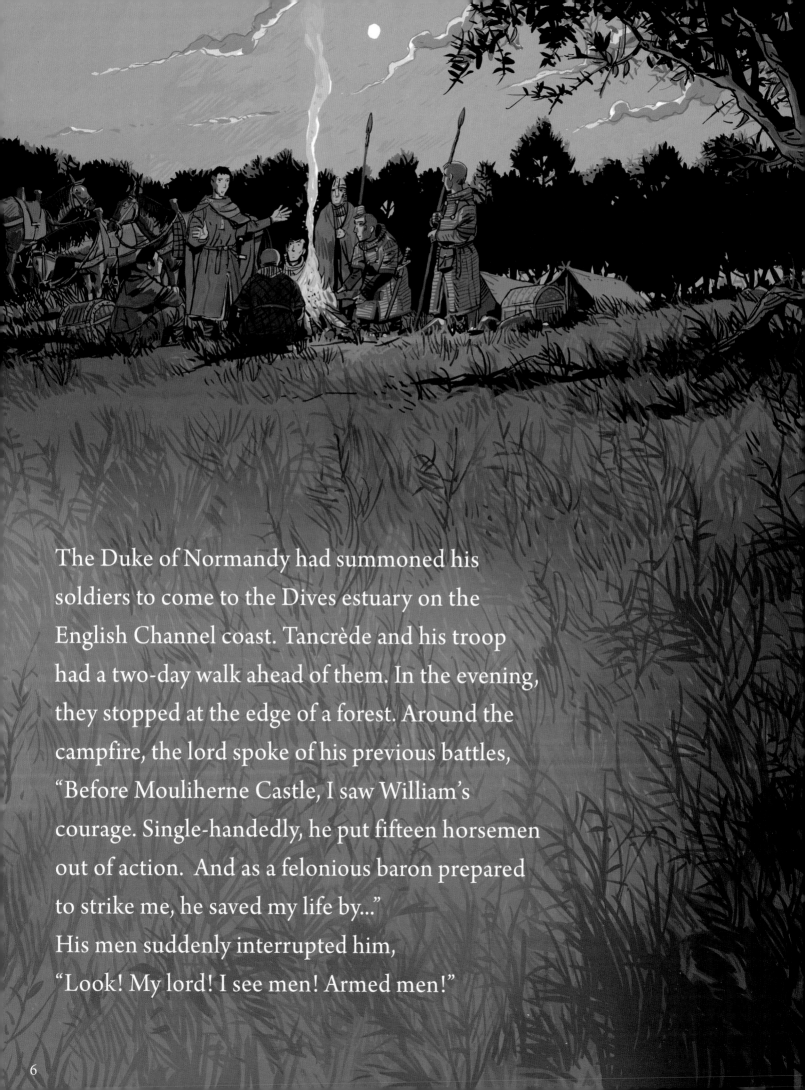

The Duke of Normandy had summoned his
soldiers to come to the Dives estuary on the
English Channel coast. Tancrède and his troop
had a two-day walk ahead of them. In the evening,
they stopped at the edge of a forest. Around the
campfire, the lord spoke of his previous battles,
"Before Mouliherne Castle, I saw William's
courage. Single-handedly, he put fifteen horsemen
out of action. And as a felonious baron prepared
to strike me, he saved my life by..."
His men suddenly interrupted him,
"Look! My lord! I see men! Armed men!"

The Normans seized their spears and thrust forwards into the forest in pursuit of the fleeing silhouettes. "By Jove, death to those bandits!" They very quickly caught up with their terrified prey. A man and his son were brought before Tancrède. "Have mercy, my lord, spare these poor starving creatures! God has put me to the test. My wife is poorly and I have seven mouths to feed..." Tancrède was moved by the man's pitiful state. He decided to help him by recruiting his son.

"Be brave, Maixent, lord Tancrède is a generous man. It is an honour for you to be by his side." Heavy-hearted, the man left his young son. The next day, the troop headed for Saint-Vigor abbey, their last stopover before reaching the coast. They came across a pedlar on their way to Dinan. "Good day, sires, are you also on your way to join our good Duke William? They are flocking from all over Normandy... but also from Burgundy, Brittany, Alsace, Picardy and even Spain and Italy!"

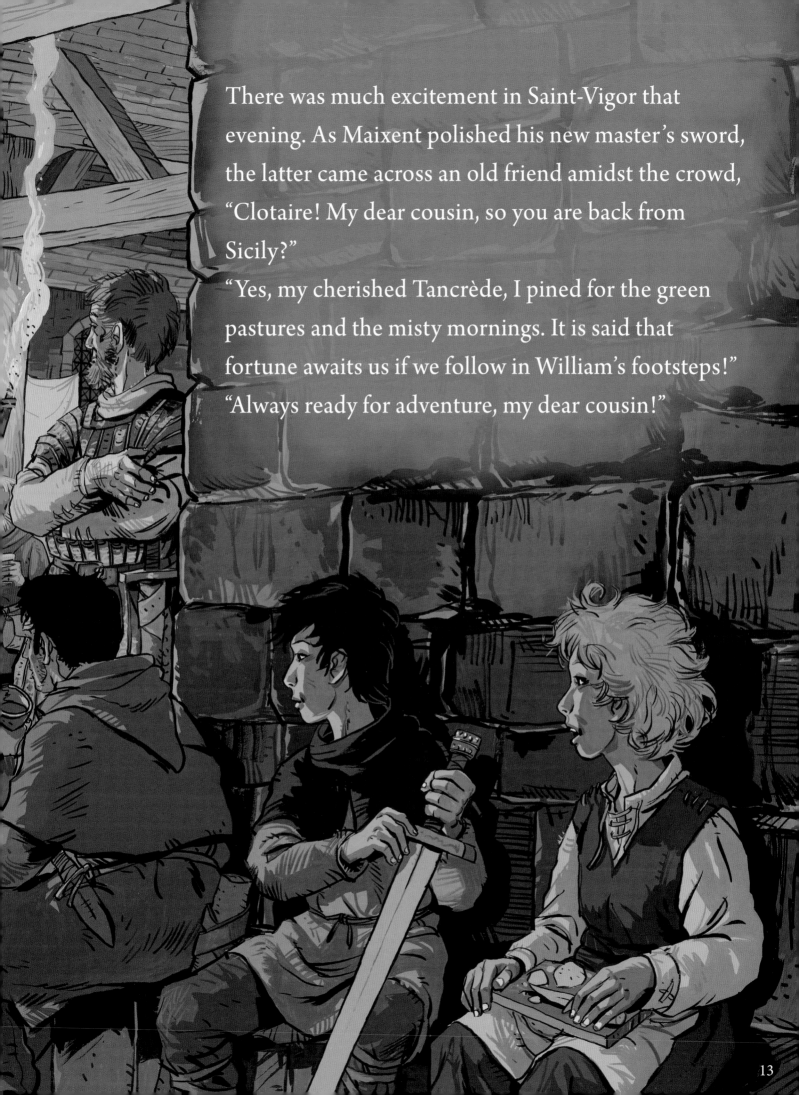

There was much excitement in Saint-Vigor that evening. As Maixent polished his new master's sword, the latter came across an old friend amidst the crowd, "Clotaire! My dear cousin, so you are back from Sicily?"

"Yes, my cherished Tancrède, I pined for the green pastures and the misty mornings. It is said that fortune awaits us if we follow in William's footsteps!"

"Always ready for adventure, my dear cousin!"

And the adventure began, indeed, at the mouth of the River Dives! Maixent set eyes for the first time on the seafront, literally invaded by the immense army. It was like an anthill. Lumberjacks had chopped down trees in the nearby forests.

Carpenters were working twice as hard to build the many embarkations needed. The boats were to be of all sizes! Since time was short, ships were also bought or hired. William was keen to take advantage of the summer months to launch his troops' assault on the English coast.

However, he would have to wait, for the winds were unfavourable. In the meantime, Clotaire told tales of his Mediterranean feats before a captive audience,

"I had left Cotentin to head for Italy, where I served rich princes. Just a few Normans were brave enough to scour those blistering lands. So many times, I fought against the Byzantines in Apulia and against the Moors in Sicily! In Lipari, I found myself a sweet wife, but despite the tender nights and the beauty of the arid countryside, I could not abandon my own family..."

As time went by, William's men grew impatient. They became angry; they quarrelled. Tancrède and Maixent had trouble keeping the latter's fiery cousin Clotaire in check,

"In the name of devil, when are those winds going to turn and lead our boats into Saxon lands?"

In August, William the Bastard left his castle in Bonneville to take up residence amidst his men, to encourage them. Maixent finally set eyes on the Norman chief,

"My lord Tancrède, look ahead, it's our duke! He is so great! William, William!"

Early September, finally taking advantage of westerly winds, the fleet sailed to Saint-Valery, a port slightly closer to the English coast. Then came a long period of bad weather with a succession of heavy rain and storms. The Duke of Normandy decided to ask for God's help. The Saint Valéry relics were carried over a procession.

Could their prayers have been heard?

On the 28th of September, Maixent announced the good news,

"God has heard our plea! Look at the banner, the winds are blowing from the south, a miracle!"

William gave immediate orders to embark.

Over twelve hours, there was much excitement and noise among the eight thousand soldiers as they loaded barrels of wine and drinking water, along with shields, helmets, spears, food, swords, bows and arrows. Maixent prepared Tancrède's horse and took it to the boats; six hundred vessels transported the horses and four hundred were reserved for the horsemen, archers and foot soldiers.

The boats sailed past the Hourdel headland at dusk. They followed William's boat, the *Mora*, which was equipped with a lantern at the top of its mast.

Great tension reigned throughout.

Most of the men embarked to face seasickness for the very first time. Maixent was no exception and he vomited his last meal. Much to the amusement of Clotaire, a hardened seaman, "How generous our young recruit is to give food to the fish! You'll need more strength than that against the Saxons!"

On the morning of the 29th of September 1066, William's army landed at Pevensey. The archers were the first to touch English soil for they were to offer cover to the horses who followed. Yet, there was not an enemy in sight. All was calm.

Barely had the Norman chief set foot on solid ground when he stumbled and fell on the beach.

Tancrède rushed to help, as Clotaire anxiously announced,

"It's a bad omen! May God protect us!"

"You are wrong, horseman - I have seized this earth with my own hands, it is ours henceforth!" William exclaimed.

The Duke of Normandy decided to wait for Harold in a town named Hastings. Indeed, the Saxon chief was busy in the north fending off the Norwegian Vikings. Informed of the Norman invasion, he was forced to reform his army and head southwards at full speed, with a quick detour via London to reinforce his ranks. In the meantime, the Normans set to fortifying Hastings.

They chased out the inhabitants,
pillaging and burning their houses.
Maixent found a good catch in
a nearby farm. "Come on porky,
if you follow me I'll introduce you to
noble Tancrède. He'll be delighted to
see me cook you on the spit for him and his men!"

Finally, on the 13th of October, the Anglo-Saxon army took up position on the hilltop a few miles from Hastings. A scout by the name of Vital sounded the alert,

"The Saxons! The Saxons! To arms!"

On the morning of the 14th, William advanced. Dry-mouthed, Maixent carried Tancrède's sword through the column of foot soldiers as they approached the battlefield. They all held their breath. The archers were the first to enter into action.

A few moments later, Maixent, who had remained to the rear on Telham Hill, watched the terrible confrontation.

Just two hundred yards away, the Saxons, protected by their shields, withstood the shock.

Maixent could see the axes brandished by the formidable Danish Housecarls, Harold's elite troops.

The Saxon lines did not break.

They even counter-attacked, pushing the Bretons on their left flank.

William then sent his powerful cavalry into battle.

At around midday, a rumour spread that the Bastard was dead. Yet, he got back up again, took off his helmet so that his men could recognise him and he spurred on his troops.

William is still alive!

Then twice more, before the resistant Saxons, the Normans pretended to retreat in a cunning trick to turn back on their enemy. The Saxons finally withdrew.

33

William ordered for his archers to fire again.

After watching his two brothers fall, Harold was in turn mortally wounded in the eye.

The Housecarls, who continued to fight, were slain to the very last man. Late afternoon, the Norman horsemen were still hounding the Saxons through the forest.

But Clotaire was down. He was wounded in the side.

"Mercy! I have been hit by a rabid rascal! What dishonour! Is my last hour upon me? Will I ever see Sicily again?"

At dusk, on that historic day, Maixent discovered the bloody battlefield on the moors of Senlac Hill. He was sure he would never forget the sight of all those dead bodies.

The Normans had taken no prisoners.

In the distance, he could see Tancrède hailing William's glorious victory with other horsemen.

"Saint Michel! *Dex aie* (God help). Victory, victory!"
The duke promised he would have an abbey built on the very spot, to give grace. Among the thousands of mutilated bodies scattered on the ground, Maixent feared discovering his master's cousin Clotaire. He set off to look for him, his stomach knotted.

He finally heard his familiar voice on the edge of a wood.

"Young Maixent, come here, help me, I can no longer walk alone!"

"Clotaire, are you bleeding? Could a Housecarl have injured you?"

"No, just a miserable peasant who surged out from behind a bush.
Let us hurry, these body robbers could well turn against us."

"Noble Tancrède is alive, and our duke is victorious, England is ours
Clotaire!"

"Then let us thank God, and may he welcome all these poor souls!"

On the 20th of October, William and his army set off towards London. They captured several towns on their way: Dover, Canterbury, Winchester.

And, on Christmas Day, William was crowned King of England in Westminster Abbey in London.

The following years were spent pacifying the kingdom. William the Bastard had become William the Conqueror.

The Battle of Hastings

On the 14th of October 1066, to the north of the town of Hastings, the King of England, Harold Godwinson's army was defeated by that of William "the Bastard", Duke of Normandy, who became master of the nation over the months that followed his victory. The Norman duke was thereafter nicknamed William "the Conqueror".

Although the Norman victory was won at a hair's breadth, Harold's death and the English defeat tragically sealed England's fate for they had huge consequences on the country's future. The year 1066 marked a major turning point in English history: henceforth, there would always be the years before and the years after that famous autumn day when the two armies confronted each other. The period that followed marked the end of Anglo-Saxon England: an elite population of Norman origin replaced the Anglo-Saxon leaders. The kingdom made a radical move from Scandinavian influence to integrate the Western European feudal system.

Harold swearing an oath of loyalty to William before returning to England. Scene 23 from the Bayeux Tapestry. Detail of the Bayeux Tapestry – 11th century - With special permission from Bayeux Town Council.

Why did this all come about?

Early 1066, on the 5th of January to be precise, the English King Edward "the Confessor" died just after consecrating Westminster abbey-church. The next day, the kingdom's noblemen met and proclaimed Edward's brother-in-law, Harold of Wessex, king. However, Duke William of Normandy was also a pretender to the throne...

King Edward was the son of Emma, one of William's great aunts. He had been brought up in exile in Normandy, hence his great love for the Normans. Around 1050-1051, Edward, who had no heir, is said

Harold crowned King of England. Scene 30 from the Bayeux Tapestry. Detail of the Bayeux Tapestry – 11th century - With special permission from Bayeux Town Council.

Guy of Ponthieu handing over his prisoner, Harold, to William. Scene 13 from the Bayeux Tapestry. Detail of the Bayeux Tapestry – 11th century - With special permission from Bayeux Town Council.

to have promised his succession to his cousin, the Duke of Normandy. Yet Harold, the powerful Earl of Wessex, had since gradually compelled recognition as the best successor thanks to his bravery and his victories in 1062-1063 against the Welsh. Nevertheless, in 1064, according to the scenes depicted on the Bayeux Tapestry, Harold travelled to Normandy for reasons that remain obscure. Taken prisoner by the Count Guy of Ponthieu, he was freed thanks to William's intervention. He then accompanied William on an expedition to Brittany before swearing an oath over holy relics. We suppose that he promised to help William to become king upon Edward's death. William left Harold to return to England with his

nephew Hakon, one of the hostages Harold's father must have entrusted to Edward in 1051. He kept the other hostage, Wulfnoth, Harold's young brother, who spent the rest of his life prisoner to the Normans!

On his death bed, Edward may well have designated Harold as his successor. According to Anglo-Saxon tradition, a will based on the deceased's last words prevails over all others. In 1066, the Duke of Normandy continued to believe in his own right as heir to the throne, as designated in 1051 and confirmed by Harold in 1064. Their confrontation was therefore inevitable...

Preparing the invasion

William was informed of Harold's coronation a few days later. The time seemed right: his father-in-law was the Count of Flanders and his two traditional adversaries, the King of France and the Count of Anjou were both still very young. He also knew he could count on support from the Church for was Harold not guilty of betraying the oath he had made in 1064? Pope Alexander II sent William the Standard of St. Peter as a sign of his support.

The Mora, *William's flagship.* Scene 38 from the Bayeux Tapestry. Detail of the Bayeux Tapestry – 11th century - With special permission from Bayeux Town Council.

The armada crossed the English Channel by night...

William convinced the Norman noblemen, along with foreign mercenaries and soldiers who flocked from all around, drawn by the potential plunder for the kingdom of England was the richest in the Western world. The Dives estuary was chosen to gather men, their horses, their equipment, material and the necessary ships for the Channel crossing.

On the 8th of September, Harold dismissed the fleet that was keeping watch over the southern English coast. The Norman fleet headed for the Somme estuary on the 12th of September pending the grand departure on the 28th. However, in the meantime, on the 18th of September, Harald Hardrada the King of Norway, who was also keen

In the Middle Ages, the Dives estuary was a vast bay. Photograph by H. Paitier, Inrap.

...to land on the beach in Pevensey the next morning. *Scene 38 from the Bayeux Tapestry. Detail of the Bayeux Tapestry – 11th century - With special permission from Bayeux Town Council.*

to seize the English throne, landed in the north of England. On the 20th, he defeated the English at Fulford, near York. Harold then rushed northwards and, on the 25th of September, obtained a crushing victory at Stamford Bridge where the Norwegian king was killed. But Harold's army had been considerably weakened in the process.

Three days later, the Normans landed without ado on the beach at Pevensey in the south of England, whilst Harold was at the opposite end of the country. William headed eastwards and established camp in Hastings, where he awaited Harold's army. The latter, who had returned to London in forced marches, rushed southwards to wage battle, without having totally reformed his army.

The walls of Pevensey Castle offered sheltered to the Normans. © Fotolia – Maciej Olszewski.

The battle

Early on the morning of the 14th of October, William set his troops in motion. He was unable to establish a position on Senlac Hill and, consequently, found himself in an unfavourable position below, with his adversaries looming above. To win the battle, the Normans needed to break through the ranks that formed a "wall of shields", comprised of the Housecarls, professional soldiers, with reinforcements comprised of men recruited on site or on the way to the battlefield.

At around 9am, around 8,000 combatants on either side found themselves face to face. The Normans boasted a cavalry force, which was not the case of the English. They also had archers and a few crossbowmen. Harold's housecarls were armed with long axes. Each side's defensive equipment was similar: an almond-shaped shield and a coat of mail.

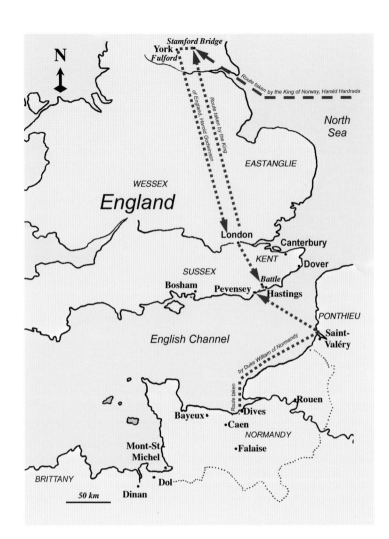

The Norman cavalry played a major role during the Battle of Hastings. © Fotolia – Thomas Owen.

The Norman horsemen facing the wall of English shields. Scene 53 from the Bayeux Tapestry. Detail of the Bayeux Tapestry – 11th century - With special permission from Bayeux Town Council.

William engaged his archers to clear the English ranks. However, their arrows bounced off the English shields. So he decided to engage the infantry, then the cavalry, whose vain assaults lasted several hours.

Late morning, William's left wing, comprised of Breton soldiers, began a disorderly retreat. At one point in the battle, William was even believed to have been killed and a wave of panic began to spread among the Normans and their allies. The duke was then obliged to remove his helmet to prove he was not dead and to rally his troops. The Normans and the Bretons immediately turned back in pursuit of the English, who had carelessly abandoned their position. The latter, now totally isolated, were massacred. The Normans successfully employed this strategy several times over the afternoon. Yet, they still hadn't succeeded in establishing a position on the ridge, in order to break through the English lines. At this point, William is said to have asked his archers to "draw high" (i.e. to shoot up in the air).

This strategy proved efficient for the English lines began to weaken and a group of Norman horsemen managed to infiltrate the English defenders and, late afternoon, to approach and kill Harold. A scene on the Bayeux Tapestry depicts Harold being hit in the eye with an arrow, then the following scene shows the English king on the ground, being finished off with swords. Panic-stricken by the loss of their chief, the English fled. By nightfall, William had achieved total victory.

The Battle of Hastings. Painting by François-Hippolyte Debon, 1844. Museum of Fine Arts, Caen. Photograph by M. Seyve.

Preparations for the conquest and the course of the battle revealed William's great qualities as a strategist and chief. Harold was an unquestionably talented military chief, as proven by his capacity to maintain a unified and orderly troop over the long hours of incessant Norman assaults. His rapid intervention combined with the element of surprise that had offered him the advantage at Stamford Bridge had failed at Hastings. But fatigue amongst his soldiers and archers in insufficient numbers very probably contributed towards his defeat.

Epilogue

After the English chiefs submitted to him, William was crowned King of England on Christmas Day in the year 1066 in the church of Westminster Abbey, near London.

To repent of the death of so many men, William later decided to have Battle Abbey built on the very spot where the battle had taken place. Today, the abbey's ruins commemorate the day the kingdom's fate took a very different turn. A stone slab located where the since disappeared church altar once stood is said to mark the spot where Harold was killed.

Ruins of Battle Abbey, built by William in 1070. © Fotolia – Tony Baggett.

The Bayeux Tapestry offers a precious testimony of the Norman Conquest by William the Conqueror in 1066 and contributed towards his glory. The embroidery, which measures 68.3 m in length for a height of 50 cm, depicts the events that preceded the Battle of Hastings and the course of the battle itself. It was very probably commissioned by the Bishop of Bayeux, Odo of Conteville, William the Conqueror's half-brother. It is believed to have been produced in England. Today, it can be admired in the "Guillaume-le-Conquérant" (William the Conqueror) centre in Bayeux, in Normandy.

It is listed, since 2007, on Unesco's Memory of the World register.

Battle Abbey entrance porch. © Fotolia – Michael Gray.

ISBN 978-2-8151-0295-7 – © OREP Éditions 2016